Preface

The history of the US has had a very ugly and brutal past and to the reader he or she may call into question my authority on my work of papers that are in the following pages, but I can tell you that I have an Associate degree in American Studies and my orgins begin in the Cherokee nation which has a brutal history itself. The only thing that I am trying to establish is my work is to show how I interpreted the information that was given to me by my professors. This brutal history begins with the removal of peoples off of their land and the Europeans who came to "claim" land as theirs and have treated Native Americans as less than human. In my research, I have not gone that far back in history to dispute that theory. But for now, in this book they are found to be farmers and hardworking individuals, from all parts of the nation of American Indians. This book also has an index of the American Timeline and my sited sources, some are already in the research papers themselves but others I sited in my works sited page

I started my studies at Fresno City College at the age of 42 years of age. I realized that there was not much of advancement in the job that I held at the library in Fresno CA. I also came to the conclusion that unless I got some kind of degree or got some college units behind me I would not succeed in life but to shelve books for the rest of it; so I enrolled in to what I called the greatest adventure of my life. The American timeline that is at the end of this book does not show everything including today's ugly history, but it reflects the many things that did actually happen from the first known peoples of this nation. I got this information from the many books and information that I have learned through the course of my studies at FCC. I cannot take responsibility for any inaccurate information that was left out nor can I take responsibility for the misguided information that was put in by the story tellers that wanted only a "white history". If the reader has any information to add that is up to the individual. I will not delete any information because of false accusations made by the reader themselves. Therefore, it is my intention to inform the reader not give guidance to the individual who may dispute the American timeline. I also will not adjust it in anyway, the reader may contact me upon its content, so we can discuss it accuracy. This can be done at <u>lindagardner2012@gmail.com</u> or facebook.com there you will find that there are posting boards and I will respond with a kind enough answer to your question or questions.

Lastly, I hope that you will enjoy reading this collection of stories and thank you for not taking anything to heart during your reading of this book. Again, Thank you. *Linda Gardner*

Linda L. Gardner was born in Fresno California and is currently writing her first collection of Native American Stories. She completed an Associate degree in American Indian Studies and Cultural Studies. She is currently at Fresno State University to complete her bachelor's degree in American Indian Studies and Fashion Merchandising. she lives in Fresno California.

Contents

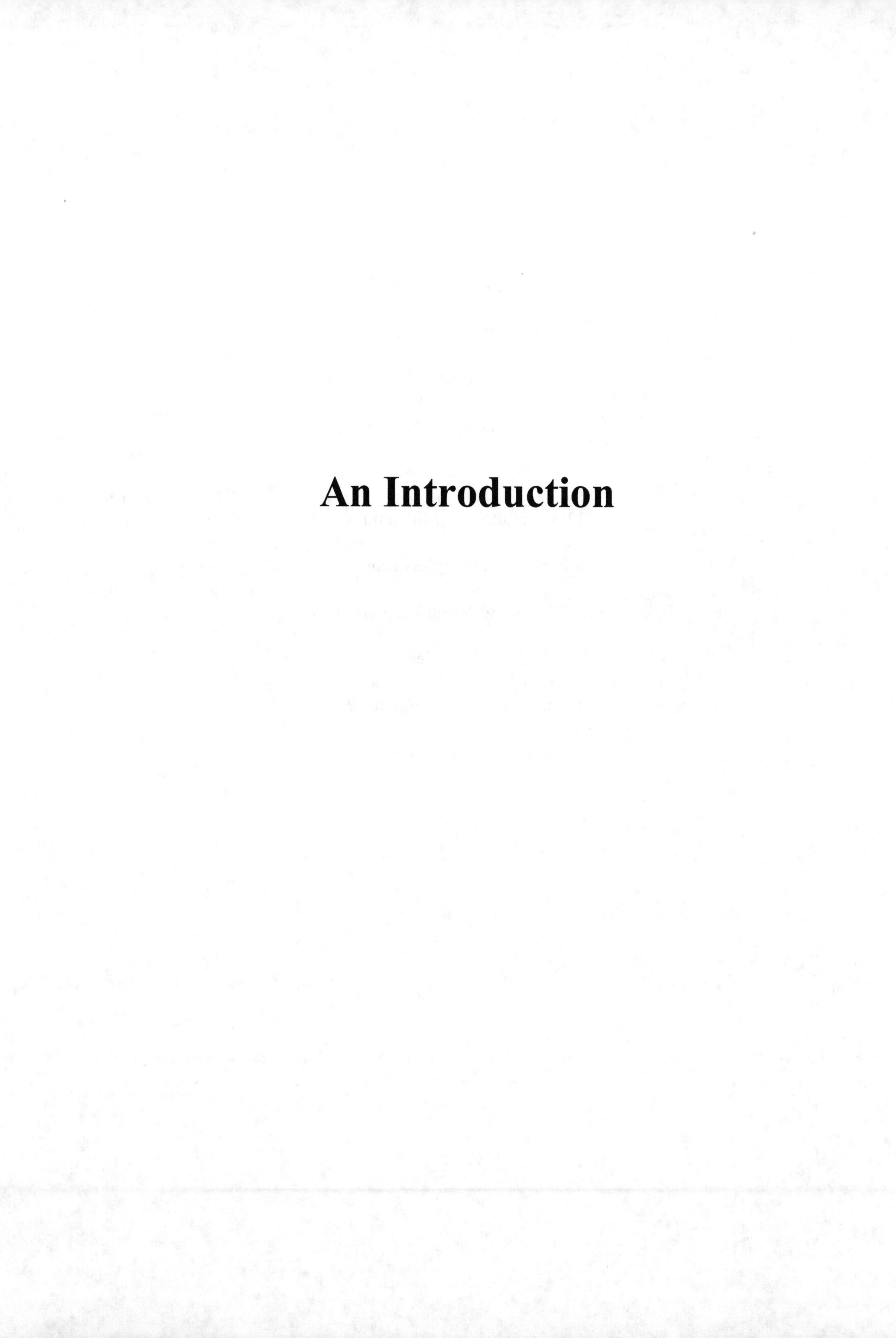

An Introduction

American Frontier 1773-1865

In the year 900 BCE-1089 Native Americans roamed this nation. There were reported to be 500 nations each with their own culture context and with their own "life ways". Life was good among each civilization they lived at peace among themselves. From 1090 to roughly 1100 there were declines in populations. It would be another 100 to 491 years before one man stepped onto this nation and try to wipe out indigenous people out.

With the signing of the Declaration of Independence in 1776, we declared independence from British Rule. Land was being explored so that settlement of the colonies could be expanded; settlers wanted to move to other parts of the nation. During the 1790's it was an eventful year. The first census was taken in the United States and war was going to escalate between the United States and Spain over land. As 1794 closed 1795 would be an important year for the Gordon's, they were a family that had come over as part of the king's debtor program. In 1773 James Gordon was born in Georgia and Nancy his wife was also born in Georgia in 1778, they met and got married in 1795.

During this period America was reshaping itself, and exploration and surveying of new lands became a possibility for many who saw this as an opportunity to go and build somewhere else. Mississippi was "Created" in 1798 from land that was taken from the Choctaw and the Chickasaw Indians, they were the first on this land. In 1798, the United States and Spain signed a treaty mapping out the Mississippi territory. The first counties that were established in Mississippi were Adams and Jefferson, founded both in that same year. They knew Indian nations lived on the land, but they still went ahead and mapped out the area anyway. The new area was "created" as new lands were cleared, there were people ready to move on these lands and take over (white European settlers) and develop it. Sales of lands would be "disputed" because of over lapping by Spain, Georgia and France. Some owners were doubtful of legality

Although Mississippi would not be an official state until 1817 it was important to establish these so people could settle into the new territory as soon as other land was available. The federal government established ordinances so that people can own property outright; the laws began with the Northwest Ordinance of 1787 & the Land Ordinance of 1798, it says:

"A Long and Varied History"

"The BLM's roots go back to the Land Ordinance of 1798 and the Northwest Ordinance of 1787 these laws provided for the survey and settlement of the lands that the original 13 colonies ceded to the Federal government after the War of Independence" As additional lands were acquired by the United States from Spain, France and other countries Congress directed that they be explored, surveyed and made available for settlement. In 1812, Congress established the General Land Office in the Department of the Treasury, to oversee the disposition of these federal Lands. As the 19th century progressed, and the Nation's land base

In 1805 an act proposed by Congress would move indigenous peoples to reservations. The Indian Removal Act enacted by congress enforced the removal, the U.S Calvary made sure the removal took place, on the orders of the United States government. Over the next three decades Mississippi was seeing changes in the way it was shaping up to become what it is today. As 1850 rolls forward it wasn't until 1852 that 61 counties were either founded or established in Mississippi; With the establishment of counties and homesteads onto Indian land, the final land act also known as the "script warrant act" would be in1855. This act allowed people one last chance to purchase property by veterans who have not had the chance to do so.   The Script warrant act of 1855 was designed to give soldiers and their families land, land for which they can settle after the war. In a lecture series by Colletta, John he states:

> Qualified applicants were given a certificate for a specific number of acres, usually 160. This certificate was also called a warrant. The selection of a parcel of land within the geographic area designated by the applicable law was called locating the warrant. Once the land was selected, the veteran or his widow or other heir received a patent for the selected parcel and surrendered the warrant back to the U.S government.

Homesteading was a lot different it allowed persons who wanted to claim land at $6.00, this fee could be paid to build a home, improve the land and plant crops. The man or woman who paid that fee was allotted 160 acres, they also had to stay on that land for 5 years. After the five years ended they owned it until it was handed down into their family or sold to pay off debts.

Foreign born citizens could purchase land, but they had to become naturalized Americans. They were called "entry men, hundreds of thousands of Sweden's, Norwegians and Danish took advantage of this offer" Credit vouchers were issued to those who wish to buy land but did not have the money up front; much like the debtors of the new colony Georgia. Georgia was the last of the new colonies to be established in the eastern part of the United States. As part of the new colony seven counties were formed to establish a barrier so that if Spain attack that area it would be defended. The seven counties are Burke, Camden, Chatham, Glynn, Liberty, Richmond & Wilkes were all formed on February 5, 1777 most are on the ocean side of the state. The new peoples to the area received 50 acres of land to pay off their debts to the English government.

The registered owner held credit vouchers, the person who wishes to buy that land would work, live and take care of it; promising to pay the amount specific to the amount agreed upon. The federal government handled these transactions through the general land office. These ordinances were enforced and if the credit voucher was not paid up, then the land was returned to the creditor. There were over 1 million people in the new colony, and land was needed to accommodate the need of the population that was growing and so that is why people wanted to establish new territories. This decade would be filled with changes on the interior of the American landscape. After Mississippi got out of the Civil war in January of 1861, more than a quarter of the soldiers who went to war, did not come home; those who did come home came home to devastation" Those who came from the north picked up the pieces of the devastation and rebuilt the area. Widows found new husbands to marry; communication and transportation systems were down or "destroyed" they were rebuilt as well.

Mississippi was rebuilt from the ashes that were left from the aftermath of the war. The decision to pull from the union was that the "States rights, not Slavery" was the decision to leave. Two societies emerged around this time the "Yeomen" who were considered "Frugal" and the "planters" who were considered to "control the states politics". The economic occupation in Mississippi was cotton, and it is considered a "Cash Crop" cotton was the major source of income among many plantation owners had slaves on those plantations to harvest that cotton; many counties were considered to grow this crop for profit.

This agriculture spans 17 states "and is a Major crop in 14" of those states cotton was picked by hand, usually by blacks. Whites joined in only because there was a shortage of labor after the civil war, of course, those plantations were reduced because some farmers with land did not have any sons to work on that land. By this time, twenty-three treaties would be signed between the Chickasaw, Choctaw and the U.S Government; these treaties only worked in the favor of the United States. Mostly these treaties were meant to end the war's that the government and indigenous people were having, and they resulted in the U.S diminishing the lands of the "First peoples of this nation". Many Nations were promised money for these lands that the U. S was taking, that money and territory would be handed over to the Bureau of Indian Affairs office of the Department of the Interior in Washington DC. Once again, the indigenous population would get the raw end of the deal, the land and money as it turns out is gone and the BIA spent it out right. As 1862 came to a close there was destruction that would strike the Shoshoni in 1863. The Bear River Massacre took place on a cold early morning raid by colonel Patrick Edward Connor and about 200 California volunteers. After young men of the Shoshoni "Struck out at the white settlers" for moving into the cache Valley in the spring of 1860. The "Mormon farmers" as they were known "appropriated all of the land and water of the Verdant mountain valley".

This was "Indian land" Chief bear hunter gathered 450 Shoshoni to make sure they would not take any more of the land. With mounting pressure, Utah officials called upon Connor and his troops to "punish the Northwestern band". "Before the colonel led his men, he vowed to take no prisoners." Silence was broken in the early morning as the Shoshoni slept.

Colonel and his men "fired indiscriminately" into the camp where they slept. When the smoke subsided, 250 Shoshoni women and children lay dead or dying. As they did so the men went through "raping women and children who were already dying from their wounds" Chief bear hunter and his sub chief Lehi were killed in this bloody battle. The same men stole 1,000 bushels of wheat and flour and they burned 75 structures and took one hundred and seventy Shoshoni horses in the aftermath of the killing spree.

As 1864 was about to end the interior of the American Frontier would get even bloodier; with more victims of the Cheyenne nation. They would fall to their deaths in November of 1864. Whether it was in response to what happened to the Shoshoni in 1863 in Utah, 600 Southern Cheyenne, Arapahos, Sioux, Comanche's, and Kiowa's from Colorado and Kansas "went on a defensive war path" their leader would be Chief Black Kettle Leader of the Cheyenne nation. The Sand Creek Massacre took place on November 29th, 1864 in Colorado.

The 600 men faced 700 men made up of the third Colorado Calvary who were mostly volunteers; men who wanted to join, led by Colonel John Chivington. The territory was Arapaho & Cheyenne "hunting grounds" in which "White developers wanted to put settlements on and develop the land for profit". The Cheyenne and Arapaho "Refused to sell their lands and settle on reservations". Colonel Chivington and the third Calvary were brutal in their attacks on the indigenous people especially the women and the children. The women were cut open; babies were taken from the womb and "clubbed" with the "butt" of the men's riffle. Children were scalped and "beaten, until their brains came out" they were "mutilated in ever since of the word" This atrocity was left with 200 dead mostly women and children. Colonel Chivington was "denounced, forced to resign" and he was considered "heartless".

He was once quoted as saying "the perfect cause for Indian extinction" and "nits make lice: reference to what he and his men did to the killing of women and children. Once a man of the clergy, he betrayed his beliefs, "his compassion for his fellow man didn't extend to the Indians".

It was indeed a horrific ordeal for Native Americans during this short time period, the tragedy that was dealt with was such a loss of life for their nations. Throughout history this has been repeated time and time again, inflicted on this culture that it is no wonder that the people responsible thought that they could eliminate the whole culture itself; but they did not. That same mentality that drove those men onto the land and claimed it as theirs to take and conquer the people who have lived here for generation after generation before white Europeans landed on the continent of Haiti 500 years ago. The superior complex of a man who thought that he could conquer the people with little or no resistant, well he was wrong.

Those who came after him were just as naïve to think the same as he did was a foolish thing. Through conquest they must take away the spirit of that person, then there is the rapping of the body and then the final act is to kill that person

to get the others to corporate. In doing so they set themselves up to look

nothing but monster; but in the history books they are heroes of our country.

This kind of eradication of culture would never be forgotten by their people,

but the stories and memories still live on it will never die out. Instead what

happened at Sand Creek and Bear River, is a lesson to us all that hate has no

place in the "Human spirit" of life itself.

Sources: **(1)** Eichholz, Alice Ph.D. Ancestry's Red Book "American State County &
Town Sources" edited c.1989 state researched Alabama by Paluzzi, Mary Bess
Ancestry Publishing Company **(2)** Gardner, Linda AA in American Indian Studies "My
American History timeline 900 before the common era and beyond" **(3)** Colletta, John
Philip Ph.D. "discovering your roots: An Introduction to Genealogy" eight session
Genealogy courses hosted by the Fresno County Genealogy Society in Fresno Ca.
Lecture four "Military and Homesteading" pgs. 4 &5
(4) Cotton.org/pubs/cotton counts/fieldtofabric/harvest.cpm Article by cotton counts
"Crop production: Field to Fabric" **(5)** blm.org/wo/st/en/info/About BLM/History.htlm
(6) Madisen, Brigham D Utah history encyclopedia book called "Shoshoni Frontier and
the Bear River Massacre" c 1985 **(7)** Lastofindependents.com/sand creek "Sand creek
massacre **(8)** Southern Cheyenne November 29th, 1864" written by unknown website is
www. native. net

Early Papers and Assignments

American Indian Movement: History in the making

What I am attempting to do in this paper is to show you the progression in which AIM was founded.

In the beginning of the American Indian Movement there were obstacles to overcome so that there could be a clear path for Indigenous people to govern their own land. Laws such as:

Worcester v. Georgia (1832)

The United States Supreme Court decided that the state had no authority over persons and actions within the boundaries of the Cherokee Nation, and that state laws did not extend to Indian Country. The ruling clarified that Indian tribes were under the protection of the federal government and that congress, and not states had plenary or overriding power regarding Indian tribes. (#2 of power point lecture on Societies American Indian Studies)

Several years passed, the Fort Laramie Treaty of 1851 was enacted, which the federal government did not keep their end of the bargain:

Fort Laramie Treaty of (1851)

September 17, 1851
Articles of a treaty made and concluded at Fort Laramie, in the Indian Territory, between D. D. Mitchell, superintendent of Indian affairs, and Thomas Fitzpatrick, Indian agent, commissioners specially appointed and authorized by the President of the United States, of the first part, and the chiefs, headmen, and braves of the following Indian nations, residing south of the Missouri River, east of the Rocky Mountains, and north of the lines of Texas and New Mexico, viz, the Sioux or Dahcotahs, Cheyennes, Arrapahoes, Crows, Assinaboines, Gros-Ventre Mandans, and Arrickaras, parties of the second part, on the seventeenth day of September, A.D. one thousand eight hundred and fifty-one. (a)
ARTICLE 1. The aforesaid nations, parties to this treaty, having assembled for the purpose of establishing and confirming peaceful relations amongst themselves, do hereby covenant and agree to abstain in future from all hostilities whatever against each other, to maintain good faith and friendship in all their mutual intercourse, and to make an effective and lasting peace.

Indigenous people had to once again defend themselves, only two years passed by then the public law legislation was passed and there would be more in affect to better assist them in protecting their reservations

Public law 280 Congressional Act (1953)

Transferred jurisdiction over most tribal lands to state governments in California, Oregon, Nebraska, Minnesota, and Wisconsin, and Alaska was added in1958. It provided that any other state could assume such jurisdiction by passing a law or amending the states constitution (#1 Colonialism Lecture 2 Am Ind 34 Societies, B. Navarro's class 2010).

As frustration began to mount because misuse and abuse of the intent of what this law was meant to accomplish went unnoticed by the ones who were supposed to enforce it; this law failed to protect the rights of women on the reservation. In the early 1960's protest became sometimes violent, they became frustrated because nothing was being done by the Bureau of Indian Affairs to help them with financial allotments, getting more land allocated etc. Protests such as the civil rights movement in Alabama among many African American's and Latino's, showed Native American's that this was the only way that their voice could be heard.

As the 50's wore on more frustration mounted, with the government wanting to relocate all of the Native Americans on reservations, some felt that they were leaving only temporary.   This act was to steal their land and resources from them, and that is what ultimately happened. What the Relocation Act of 1956 did to Native Americans was:

The relocation Act of 1956 resulted in more than half of the 1.6 million Indians in the U.S.A to relocate to urban centers signing agreements to not to return to their respective nations/reservations in the future. (Churchill and Morris 16) today 97.5 percent of the aboriginal land base, and its resources has been confiscated by the U.S and Canadian governments (Churchill and La Duke 243) the internal colonization of first nations peoples, even if discussed infrequently is indeed prominent and currently existing. (http://siouxme.com/lodge/land.html)

Native Americans lost out in the deal because their land base shrunk, and resources were taken and sold off by the government, many had no choice but to try and to survive in urban areas of the cities. However, many Indigenous peoples have returned to the reservations only to find more poverty and third world conditions.

Indian Civil Rights Act (1968)

This Congressional act revised Public Law 280 by requiring states to obtain tribal consent prior to extend and legal jurisdiction over an Indian reservation. It also gave most protections of the Bill of Rights and the Fourteenth Amendment to tribal members in dealings with their tribal governments. (#1 Colonialism Lecture 2 AmInd 34 Societies, B. Navarro's class 2010).

Indian tribes were granted sovereignty on their reservations, "Urban Indians" formed an "Indian Patrol" AIM- (American Indian Movement) led by young Native Americans, such as Dennis Banks, George Mitchell, Herb Powers, Clyde Bellecourt, Harold Goodsky, and Russell Means.

One of their beliefs was "that direct militant confrontation with the US government was the only way to redress historical grievances and to gain contemporary civil rights" (Quote from power point presentation B. Navarro's Class Am Ind. 34). The only recourse that they thought that they had to do and that was to seize Alcatraz Island in 1969. That was just a start for AIM; in the early 70's bigger movements were planned and carried out by the young "Urban Indians". With the seizure of the Pacific Gas & Electric River Dam in Redding California 73', Wounded Knee 74-75', and the occupation of the Bureau of Indian Affairs in Washington DC 75'-76', known as the Trail of Broken Treaties March, AIM set out to get their message across that they were here, and they wanted government blood.

Clyde Bellecourt is quoted "We are not free. We do not make choices; our choices are made for us; we are poor" these words were spoken at the President's National Commission on Rural Poverty in 1969.

What AIM accomplished was:
1. Reversal of the Federal termination policy
2. Adoption of Self-determination policies through passage of several statutes
3. Renewal of and recommitment to tribal traditions which specifically resulted in the following:
   a. Repatriation of many Indian ancestral remains;
   b. Flourishing of American Indian art and cultural organizations
   c. Growth of tribal Language programs and tribally-controlled education;
   d. Reconnection and re-affiliation of many Indian peoples with their traditional communities (Dr. Bernard Navarro Ph.D. Sociology Fresno city college lecture power point on AIM)

By the 1990's AIM took on a more diplomatic role than before, what came out of it was the "Red Power" movement which showed that you do not need violence to get what you want; the goals of this movement were as follows:
1. Self-determination and an end to the entire-trustee-ward relationship between the federal government and Indian nations;

2. Federal support for tribal traditions and sovereignty

3. Improved living conditions and justice for all Indian peoples.

Basically, what it comes down to is either being terminated v being free, Native American's should be free to make their own choices and to be treated just like you and me they have no special power. They are well educated Indigenous medical doctors, lawyers, Professors and blue-collar workers who want to be treated with respect. With rising employment and crime rates, many reservations are trying to break out of that poverty cycle, so they can be self sufficient and reverse the stereotypes that have been placed upon them for centuries.   The one thing that they still want to see is the end of racism; one can assume that this is what all peoples of this nation want to see one day. Racism is in the minds of those who speak it, and when they find out the truth (one day soon I hope) they will realize that it can be overcame and all people can unite together for the benefit of all cultures around the world.

Reference Sources

1. Navarro, Bernard Dr. Ph.D. of Sociology and Professor of American Indian Studies-American Indian Studies 34 Class Spring of 2010 Lecture-power point on colonialism pg 3

2. Navarro, Bernard Dr. Ph.D. of Sociology and Professor of American Indian Studies-American Indian Studies 34 Lecture –power point pages 5-7

3. Web Source http://www.canku-luta.org/PineRidge/laramie_treaty.html

4. Web search: History 2800/WK 9 Women & Politics II/Uleth-Spring 2001 "Women's Political Activism and Red Power"

5. "Incantation to Dispel New Age Dogma" From News from Native California (Summer 1999) by Parris Butler (C) pg 185 of Native American Voices by Lobo, Susan, Talbot, Steve 2001

6. Relocation Act of 1956 web address (http://siouxme.com/lodge/land.html)

"By Golly" A Biography of Vine Deloria Jr

As philosophers go Vine Deloria Jr. is only known to the indigenous

nations of this world. Little of him is known to outsiders, why because

there are no books written about him but many books are written by him

such as *Red Earth, White Lies* by fulcrum books, *Custer died for your*

sins, God is Red. My American Indian Studies teacher introduced me to

his book *Spirit and Reason* last fall semester and from the first

assignment I was hooked, we had three more assignments that semester

and I completed all three even the other assignments I read and

completed, I absorbed everything as I always do when I get introduced

to great reading material or to a subject.

"The author wants us the readers to know how important scared places are to Native
Americans. It is their struggle to keep these places such as the "Black Hills" in South
Dakota from being destroyed by non-Native Americans. He also wants us to care
about the land in which we live on, to protect it against destruction. By Native
Americans taking a stand against the government taking what they see as their land
instead of it once belonging to Native Americans, they (Native Americans) are
protecting vital traditions and religious practices. For them it's a way of life that will be
handed down for generations to come. Instead of the old ways in which Native
Americans have lived for so many years they must learn new ways of living in order to
survive, therefore lands are being overpopulated and crowed to the point where we
must expand onto places where many generations ago were once thought of as spiritual
places and are still considered so today. We as people of any background should
protect what resources that are left and stop polluting the land in which we live on for
our future generations to come or we won't have any left to protect".

*(1) (From Journal #3 assignment in American Indian Studies 31, Mr. Bernard Navarro Ph.D. in Sociology,
Chapter 26- Scared Place and Moral Responsibility by Vine Deloria Jr)

These kinds of thoughts are the exact thing that Mr. Deloria brings out in

me; I have no formal training or anything. When reading his works you can only imagine yourself as an ingenious person, putting yourself in the shoes of a Native person you feel compelled by their struggle to attain a place in this world just like you and I are entitled to have. From what I have read already and have heard from others Vine Deloria is an eloquent speaker and philosopher. I know that I am way out of my element when it comes to this one man, to whom I have never met or will even meet. I know that there are many great speakers and one can train them-selves to speak eloquently but that eludes me even to this day. Born in 1933 on the Pine Ridge Sioux Reservation and the son of Dakota Episcopal priest his father took him to the site of the 1890 Wounded Knee massacre where his father pointed out to him some survivors who still lived there. For awhile he wanted to follow in his father's footsteps but learned the "Importance of building a national power base for Indians through grassroots organizing" (2)

Bibliography

1. Journal assignments #3 & #7 by Linda Gardner done in American Indian Studies 31 Mr. Bernard Navarro Instructor Fall of 2008

2. An article Where the buffalo go: how science ignores the living world: an interview with Vine Deloria Jr. Published in "The Sun" July 2000

3. Spirit & Reason the Vine Deloria Jr. Reader by Vine Deloria himself 1999, Indian philosophy, social conditions and study, teaching.

Indians today

Vine Deloria Jr. Use's rhythm and humor to deliver a wonderful story telling delivery of his opinion, he also has a serious tone. He touches on the behavior of the Anthropologist who knowingly sees only what he/she wants to and thus prints that knowledge in his or her book, if only the "five-thousand-dollar secretary" translates it correctly. Add humor and seriousness to this and this chapter spells out that Indigenous people are human, and they deserve the respect that truly they have not been given at any point in the history of this world, I am sure that sometime some people have thought they have given more than that but truly it has not been there.

The first quote page100 that stays in mind is "Karma grinds slowly" to me this means that what comes around goes around, and it is true if you mess with someone. Karma comes back and bites you straight in the butt, so don't mess with Karma.

The second quote page81 "A warrior killed in battle could always go to the happy hunting grounds "I think what he trying to show us here is that the difference a noble fighter and a person who just sits on his or her duff and takes notes is that if you are prepared to fight you will end up in a better place than to be exiled into a life of heck the "Happy Hunting grounds" being heaven.

The third quote page 99 "The white man will continue to take Indian land because he will feel that he is HELPING to bring civilization to the poor savage"

Explain to me how do they help? It just raises more questions I think. Given the choice between the French and Indigenous people I would gladly choice the latter.

Anthropologists should learn not to be so critical of others. Sitting there watching people is not a way to observe people of another culture. Talking to them, finding out what really is wrong in their community, listening; caring and trying to help out in some small way can possibly improve the well being of humanity. You don't have to be an Anthropologist to observe the community that surrounds you, you just have to get off your lazy duff and stand as if you are a tree and watch people as they inter act with others and maybe you will understand that we are a part of this life and that we should pitch in and help.

I can put myself into the shoes of the anthropologist, but I would never just write about the things that I wanted to write about by this I mean the fluff. I am a natural outsider to this world, by this I can just stand there and observe people and be a part of their world as well. An example of this is my lunch crew: when I leave my American Indian 34 class I head towards the café on campus, where if given a good day my lunch crew will be there.

My lunch crew comprises of Tom, he happens to white by skin color and Joseph, Robert, and Richard whom I just met recently. They are of Hispanic origin to the trained eye; even though they are of the male species and I am of the female species, we somehow are able to get along. When we are at one table it is like we can converse at the same language, I observe them while they are talking to each other. I find myself laughing at the jokes that they so easily tell each other, and when a new person walks up to them that they know they are so easily inclined to acknowledge that person by giving them a hug as a greeting. These are my findings that this bunch of misfits-want to be-ourselves- and no one will break us from our pact lunch crew are here to stay as long as we are on this campus-and that we-know who we are and will not destroy the code of life.

Journal

When I was in college we were asked by the professor to read a selection of work by Vine Deloris Jr. and to select three quotes from the book. Here are my favorite ones. I hope that the reader enjoys them and to pick up readings from this author whose works will be passed on forever.

1st: (page 2)- "Seven Day Absents"

While still believing in a higher power myself, I myself do not identify with being a Christian because I believe that we have choices in this world and one of them is that we have the ability to think for ourselves. The point I am trying to convey in this is no matter whom you are Native American or white; we get to choose who or what we believe in.

2nd: (page 8)- "You have to actually live in it"

The "it" is life and if you don't live "it" then there is someone who will live "it" for you, we are "enslaved to a certain life" and no one really wants to trade our "material comfort" for anything. I think we can have both of which can provide us with actually living our lives and enjoying the rewards of this earth.

Let me explain: when we consume too much of a good thing we get bloated, and if we cut back and consume less we even out. If Native Americans consume too much Technology they become overwhelmed but you should never forget your way of life.

3rd: (page 12)- "Maturity: the ability to reflect on the ordinary aspects of life and discovery their real meaning"

In the "Indian experience" elders are cherished more so than anyone

because they have lived longer than the rest; that's why I feel as if my own experience has left me with the wisdom that I will carry around with me for the rest of my life. Knowledge is what we gain when life kicks us in the ass and we learn from it. Life teaches us the knowledge we experience our hardships. Acceptance, love, friends, and family are the wisdom we surround ourselves with on an everyday basis.

"Masks in the new millennium"

These are reading selections from a class assignment from when I was in my American Indian Studies classes. The author is Wynona La Duke she is a wonderful teacher and activist who strives to bring the American Indian spirit back to life through her readings. These are the ones that I thought the reader will enjoy.

Page 135: "What mascots do is trivialize and demean individuals and erase a culture"

> I like this quote because it does ring true about how we treat those
>
> who we do not know and those individuals who seem foreign to us.
>
> We always want to portray Native Americans as the savage image and
>
> barbaric type, instead we should see them as being: Fathers, mothers,
>
> caregivers and professionals who live like we do etc.

Page 144: "The exploitation for financial gain in association with a product so deadly to Indian people"

> In my opinion it is a double hit because not only Native Americans
>
> have alcohol consumption problems but they are once again being
>
> exploited for their savage ways. To exploit someone for financial gain
>
> is what most non-human beings do to gain wealth and the liquor
>
> industry did just that. You don't hear of a Wade Boggs hard liquor of
>
> Sammy Sosa wine, no you don't and you never will. It will always be
>
> the "Fighting Sioux" or the "Cleveland Indians" that will parish in our
>
> history minds.

Page 148: "In the end, it is a question of who gets to decide your identity"

This statement is true because who does get to decide any ones identity, and what the outcome of any one's life will be. Only and only then we as individuals get to decide who we really are and where we end up, no one should have to do that for us.

Poverty on reservations

Poverty on our nation's reservations affects all of us. The Sioux of South Dakota and the Cheyenne are among some of the poorest reservations here in the United States. While other reservations thrive and prosper the others have poverty rates that are staggering. Children on these lands consider where they live "a third world country" instead of living on the lands of their ancestors; which were thriving many thousands of years ago.

What does a person look like who indigenous? This person is real just like you and me but there is one difference. This person has had their land taken away from their ancestors and it has been rapped over and over again by anyone who feels that they should just take it from them and that means our government. According to one of the most quoted sayings the BIA is the "Fox guarding the hen house", which means that they are guarding 500 million dollars and counting. It has been taken by the signing of treaties this includes land that was taken from Native Americans, which rightfully belongs to their nations. As oil and other natural resources were found on aboriginal lands, the government would step in and sign treaties with Natives. The whole point was to trick them into giving up their land where they were, then they could force them to move off of the land to other parts of the state or the content. This is written in history books of what had happen to the Cherokees, these little funds are trickling down onto reservations.   They barely cover the expenses, for their families to survive; if they were to receive that money they would be the wealthiest people in our society. Where is the money today? Some have done an audit of the BIA and those funds don't exist anymore. It was said that the government used them for roads and such for states that needed the money, but what really happened to it? I can only guess and say it went into the hands of those who wanted to party or saw it as a slush fund for their pockets.

There are several sides to every story and this proposal is just that a proposal. The topics that are going to be discussed in this proposal are and not including:

Should we give back more land to Natives
Is our government committing genocide against Native Americans?
What is the crime rate on reservations? And how can it be stopped or prevented?
Does the BIA have the money to help reservations out of their money troubles?

Opposition to these questions are:

Is there enough growth and development to make reservations thrive on their own?
Does there need to be more protection laws for Natives?
Is there enough services that can be provided to help out people on reservations, or should there be more services that need to be available so that Natives feel as if someone out there cares?

Our government is committing genocide against indigenous people already more so than any other culturally diverse people.

Proof of this comes from information from several articles written by Native American's themselves, in one powerful article which was given to me in an assignment to read and to summarize for class; it is called *Soul Wound*. In President Ulysses S. Grant 's 1869 "Peace Policy" it forced 100,000 Native Americans into boarding schools where they were stripped of their heritage and of their languages which they were forced to forget.

If they did use their language they were punished, those lasting effects linger still today in the next generation of those who have survived; they have been told of their struggle to survive and how they will never forget who they were supposed to become.

In the next article and more proof of the government's attempt to dismantle the people of this land is in Liane Hansen's article "Native languages "A major goal of our governments various policies including boarding schools and urban relocation, was aimed at eliminating native languages, but through efforts of many tribes they are bringing back their native scared languages that were lost because of the governments forced assimilation period". Urban relocation is described as moving off of the reservation and into urban areas so they Native American's can take advantage of the resources that the government provides.

On reservations-Crime, Violence, Alcoholism and Poverty.

Since the incident at wounded Knee in the late 70's crime, violence, alcoholism and poverty have been ramped there even more so than ever before, now there is a greater need for more security and funding to help native Americans achieve self-determination according to two articles the first one is by Meghann M. Cuniff title "Police seek help in solving racial attacks" and the second one is by Carrie Johnson's "Justice Dept. on Indian country crime" both are very powerful.   In Carries Johnson's article "Justice Dept." this article focuses primarily on the reservation itself; with a bill submitted for congress so more grant money for "Youth mentoring, victim assistance and crime prevention" can be allotted to reservations so "workers responsible for policing crime on the reservations" can do more to help with "overwhelmed" "grossly underfunded" workers so they will be able to assist in the prevention and deter crime before it happens.

The American Indian Movement (AIM) was formed "to oppose the intense poverty and racism Native Americans faced" (Robert S. article) as well during this period of time to control and police the reservations but more violence and deaths occurred; Two FBI agents were killed, and several bystanders were also killed in the shot out on the Pine Ridge reservation which lead to arrest of Leonard Peltier who is incarcerated for those deaths.   Pending a parole hearing he may see to live the rest of his life back on the reservation in which he was sworn to protect, because he knows who really killed those men and hopes that one day that person will confess so he can see some of his family who has been waiting patiently for his release.

Bureau of Indian Affairs is considered by many as "The fox guarding the hen house"

Background

Established in the 1789-1824's the bureau of Indian affairs first was in the war department and it was a separate bureau; 1849 it was changed to the U.S. Department of the Interior. They handled trade with Native American's; administration conflicts lead to The Dawes Act of 1887, The Burke Act of 1906, and the Wheeler-Howard Act of 1934 and now they just act as trustee over Native American lands and funds.

<u>Forward</u>

To present day and on to the suspicious activity that has landed many Native American's to protest the mishandling of money and property handled by the Bureau of Indian Affairs.

AIM members drove a caravan to Washington DC in the early 70's and took control of the BIA offices they ransacked and destroyed ancient artifacts in protest of the bureau for that mishandling of their funds. Two million dollars' worth of artifacts that were taken from Native American were destroyed by them; office equipment was destroyed as well and was replaced.

Even Today if Native Americans want or need anything on the reservations they have to ask for it from the bureau, it is as if they are "small children" asking their "father" for money and dad can say no you can't have it.

Opposition Rebuttal

Opposition: Giving back of our land to indigenous peoples of this nation would mean that we would have to leave; therefore, we should not give it back to them because it is our country too.

Growth and Development that already exists "How far we have come already" progress that has been made since we as a nationally diverse nation have made this country.

"How far we have come already" is a saying from a song that I have no clue who sang but it is true. Without the foresight of our founding fathers and the new era of the industrial revolution in the 1900's where would we be as a nation? With the development of new and evolving technology we as a nation would still be in the past clicking stones together and/or chiseling out the wheel. Without the infrastructure of what has been built already, today's technology and the advancement in medicine could not have been possible without the knowledge from the past.   The Importance of the people who have come over from other countries as well, have played a huge part in the progress we have been making towards a better tomorrow. Therefore, this country would not exist without all of us in it, the civil rights movement in Alabama to the marches in Washington on the war in Vietnam to all races wanting an equal say in how we live as people of this country.

We as American's of all walks of life are a virtual melting pot of one united peoples, so given Native American's history and knowing a few good and awesome people I know want us to share this country with them.

Establishment of laws that protect their rights as a sovereignty nation people, so they can govern themselves.

Delaware sin Treaty of 1778 Established statehood-was signed during the revolutionary war to help the government fight the British. (Notes from Bernard's Am Indian 34 class notes)

The Dawes Act of 1887-Provides land parcels to tribes and "Indian societies must and can be regenerated", another quote is "Status, responsibility and power", "Cultural and religious liberty" and that their lands must be "Used and cherished on the way the particular Indian groups desires"

The Wheeler-Howard Act of 1934- Authorized tribes to draft constitutions setting up the machinery of self-government and of Incorporation to carry on tribal economic enterprises.

Proposed Resolutions/Solutions:

Health Care -On the reservations and in urban America the government provides health care for Native American and for non-Native Americans, in fact educational programs and scholarships are available to everyone more so to minorities than any other group. It is only those who take advantage of those programs who will succeed and will continue to do so that will insure that their family and generations to come succeed and to thrive within their own nation.

According to the article "Indian health bill gain steam again" by Rob Capriccioso time is running out on new legislation to revitalize the Indian Health Care Improvement Act, which provides health care services to Native Americans and Alaska Natives "to help fulfill the U.S.

government's treaty and trust responsibilities to Indian country".

Proposed bill will do the following:

> Authorize programs to increase the recruitment and retention of health care professionals, such as updates to the scholarship programs, demonstration programs which promote new, innovative of health care, to improve access to health care for Indians and Alaska Natives.

> Authorize long-term care, including home health care, assisted living and community-based care. Current law provides for none of these forms of long-term care.

> Establish mental and behavioral health programs beyond alcohol and substance abuse, such as fetal alcohol spectrum disorders, and child sexual abuse and domestic violence prevention programs.

Full-Circle Ending All these is proposed so everyone will have a chance to thrive in their community. The health of Children, Women and Men are essential for life on the reservation if they parish then the richness dies with them and future generations will never know how rich they really are, for most non-natives see it differently than I do. With the changes of our world today and beyond the scope of life, I can only hope that we can all thrive on this planet and share in the natural beauty of what we make our own lives. For the future of generations of people who have not been born yet I would like to say that this can only be a wakeup call for those who want to achieve what life has to offer them, I wish that in the present that our government will see to it to help the Indigenous people, to provide more instead of taking more. We all should do more to help those who cannot help themselves.

Reference:

Fresno County Library site: www fresnolibrary org-Online database for the following articles:

Johnson, Carrie" Justice Department focusing on Indian county crime", Siegal, Robert "Peltier parole prospects spurs debate", Capriccioso, Rob "Indian bill gain steam again", Hansen, Liane "Your letters: Native languages/ Liane tattoo", Cuniff, Meghann M. "Police seek help in solving racial attacks" Smith, Andrea "Soul Wound: The Legacy of Native American Schools"

Research articles from the Fresno county library site database:

Delaware sin Treaty of 1778, Dawes Act of 1887, Burke Act 0f 1906, Wheeler-Howard Act of 1936

From Columbia University electronic encyclopedia 6th edition the following articles:

American Indian Movement (AIM) Reference Entry, Indian Affairs, Bureau also a Reference Entry

Additional Sources:

- Dr. Bernard Navarro Ph.D. of Sociology his power point lecture on Native America for American Indian studies 34 a class at Fresno city college
- "Indian Protest Damage $2 Million" dated 11-10-1972 & "Protesting Indians Hold onto US Building" dated 11-4-1972 articles from the Fresno Bee microfilm
- "The Canary Effect" video

Interviews with

Konkle, Michael works in and around Fresno CA, he is from the Maidu, Nation

Navarro, Bernard Dr. Ph.D. in Sociology - his family linage is from the Southern Ute nation (mostly from his mother's side) he teaches American Indian Studies and Sociology at Fresno City College since 2005

This paper was written as a proposal for fixing up our nations reservations. It is in no way to be considered a real proposal, but for guidelines that were thought up from a video called "the canary effect". The movie was shown in a church in Fresno California in the fall of 2009. My research has many depths to it and I am attempting to suggest how to generate some funds to help Native Americans to help save their cultural heritage and to preserve it for future generations. I have never stepped onto a reservation myself, maybe sometime in the future I may do so.

Scared Places and Moral Responsibility

All of the places that we see as just land are scared to Native Americans.

It is our struggle to keep these places such as the "Black Hills" in South

Dakota from being destroyed by people who see a hillside and think that

it would be a great place to put figure heads on it. We should care about

the land in which we live on, to protect it against destruction. By Native

Americans taking a stand against the government, they are standing

against what was taken from them. Also, they are protecting vital

traditions and religious practices that was stripped from them in the

boarding schools. It was a practice by the government in which they

forced young Native children to adhere to the traditions of the Christians

who ran them. For them it was a very painful way of life; until the late

1950's when the boarding schools were considered useless. The

traditions and customs are being brought back will be handed down for

generations to come. Instead of the old ways in which Native

Americans have lived for so many years they must learn new ways of

living in order to survive. Their lands are being overpopulated and

crowed to the point where we must expand onto places where many

generations ago were once thought of as spiritual places and are still

considered so today. We as people of any background should protect what resources that are left and stop polluting the land in which we live on for future generations to come or we won't have any left to protect.

I personally think as I get older that I reflect more often on how other people of any race, religion, or personal experiences they have had to struggle harder to accomplish what I have had almost given to me, no one should take for granted the opportunities that are presented to each one of us as far as education, Jobs etc. We share this world with many different cultures and that we should respect and preserve our own culture, we should not try and be someone we are not. I see many people try and incorporate themselves into other cultures it makes me sad that they can not accept themselves as who they are. I know I would never try and be someone who I am not. I have always tried to live my life to the best of my abilities and within my own culture and beliefs.

I think by recycling cans and bottles, and by doing my part in riding the bus everyday I am helping the planet in some way. By volunteering at culture events such as the Hmong New Year event at the fairgrounds one fall day towards the beginning of the year. I enrich and expand my life to understand the differences that other people have to have in order to survive. I don't take for granted what has been given to me by being born on this earth and in this life. My religious views are my own, and I was raised believing there is a higher power and that he has created this earth and the people on it, well I was wrong.

I learned otherwise, through questioning the things around me, for example:

God may exist in practice with most religions. It is up to a person to believe in whoever they want to believe in that is the kind of society we live in today's world. I am fine believing that he is there when I need him to get me through the tough times in my life.

I also believe that everything is a live and it has life to it, trees, animals, even the scared places that are living all around us today. Scared places are all around us as well, and we have a Moral responsibility to keep these places from being destroyed by ignorant people who want to build a shopping mall, so retailers can profit from those who need a pair of Nikes. The lesson is that if we keep on destroying what has been given us, then we will have nothing left for the future.

Today's Society

In today's society when you judge a person solely based upon what a person looks like you have a prejudice view of the world, I was told by many that I too am prejudice in what I believe. We need to find a way to dispel those myths and beliefs that lead to the thoughts of prejudice and make sure that we eliminate prejudice altogether.

Becky Slaton's research on "The psychology of prejudice and stereotyping" was something I paid close attention to. I think that stereotyping is ramped in our society today and will always be there, the examples she gave in class and the video we watched are some very good examples of stereotyping that exist today and will continue to exist because we tell those who don't fit into our idea of being intelligent or less of a social class than that of ourselves, by speaking our minds and our body language as well tells them that they are inadequate and they do not belong in our social class. An example of this would be a demeaning one of: the teacher would turn his/her back to them when in class, and not acknowledge their questions altogether making them feel invisible.

Some examples of the type of stereotyping that was in the video were:

A. Industrial workers, five were considered more intelligent than their counter parts. But none the less the instructor taught the whole class no differently.

B. Teachers in a typical classroom were told that 20% of the students were less likely to excel than the rest of the class and they did.

And so on, it is so typical that the school system would do that to children. Teachers believing that one race of a child would do better than another, when told that certain children were slower learners and then telling that child that he/she would not excel; it should be considered child abuse and the school system should pay the teacher's salary to the parents to whom they had said it too. But they the teacher's get away with it all the time and no one says anything, not even the child. I think that the teacher's themselves should be given a punishment when they are found out and not a slap on the wrist, for every abusive word a teacher elicits they should have to pay $20 into a jar and at the end of the semester treat the kids to a pizza party, like a swear jar.

My example in class received a passive and yet lied to answer by Becky Slaton, also I felt invisible to her and the teacher Bernard. I only bring this up because I need to address these issues as they occur. My example was from the beginning of my employment when I first started my job with Fresno County Library; when I started the very first day me and this man who got hired with me were standing together at the counter and the office assistant looked at me (without knowing me) she said that when I do not pass the final test of the employment part that we would figure out something, at the same time she looked at him and said to him that he would pass and that she wasn't worried. I ask you how you would handle the situation; I know I did everything that I could to pass that section of employment.

It just made me more determine to pass, the response was (by Becky) was to lie that what we saw in the video did not apply to my situation at all In the video was a classroom setting, but it did and then the teacher (Bernard) asked a male dominate society question to her making me feel invisible; I left the room because I had to go to work. The matter is over and done with but still the feeling of being invisible is still there, but I don't care about being brushed off I get that all the time. I know that I must work harder than the rest of the world if I want the things in life everyone else can get if they (women of a certain type) can get easier than me.

I just need to keep up with my own self-improvement and self-assurance even though things will be a challenge and that I have to keep on the right track, I will try to ask the right questions in class and hopefully I will not get treated like I am invisible when I do ask the right questions.

What does a Native American Look Like?

This paper will prove that the indigenous people of this nation are here alive and thriving. Definition of a person who is indigenous: This person is real just like you and me but there is one difference, this person has had their land taken away from them and it has been rape over and over again by everyone who feels that they should just take it. According to one of my professors the BIA are the "Fox guarding the hen house" (Interview III) which means that they are guarding over 500 million dollars and counting that belong to Native Americans. That only means that pennies on the dollar are trickling down onto reservations so indigenous people can take care of their families. If they were to receive that money they would be the wealthiest people today in our society.

Instead the Sioux of South Dakota and the Cheyenne are among some of the poorest reservations here in the United States. Children are so desperate to escape that they will find any way they can to escape that means taking their own lives; rather than having to live on the reservation itself (Canary effect). Those who live there now compare it to living in a third world country. In the concept them vs us some educators would say that this is what it has come down to in the last 400 years, plus the fact that genocide has taken place during those years. It starts out innocencely enough the looks and then the remarks that are flown out of the mouth without thinking, because someone is different than the person who is making the remark.

It is called "The Pygmalion effect" or "The Rosenthal effect" developed by *Robert Rosenthal* and *Lenore Jacobson* in 1968. This effect was the phenomenon that was placed on people to perform better in school, but within *"sociology"* it often got placed into social class. This was also to strip Native Americans of their identity and culture, thus placing this group into stereotypes known to everyone who believed in what those expectations were to be true. Is our "White" government committing genocide against indigenous people already more so than any other culturally diverse people?

Proof of this comes from information from articles written by Native American's themselves.   In one powerful handout it is called *Soul Wound* by Andrea Smith. In it President Ulysses S. Grant 's 1869 "Peace Policy" forced 100,000 Native Americans into boarding schools where they were stripped of their heritage and of their languages which they were forced to forget. If they did use their language they were punished, and going until the late 1950's so for many decades Indigenous peoples have had to suppress their Native tongue and gotten beaten for speaking it. Often time's indigenous people will marry outside their culture and those who are not Native American will not allow them to teach, speak or even have an ounce of their heritage in the home. More so in the same respect, they themselves don't want it in their homes.

In the next series of articles shows more proof of the government's attempt to dismantle the people of this land. In the article "Native languages" by Liane Hansen *"A major goal of our governments various policies including boarding schools and urban relocation, was aimed at eliminating native languages. But through efforts of many tribes they are bringing back their native scared languages that were lost because of the governments forced assimilation period".* Urban relocation is described as moving off of the reservation and into urban areas so Native American's can take advantage of the resources that the government provides. For speaking their language in the boarding school system; Native American children were punished by having to scrub the floors or worse "Their mouths were scrubbed out with lye and chlorine solutions for uttering native words" these threats were made by the priests and the nuns who were there to help. (soul wound).

Crime, Violence, Alcoholism and Poverty on reservations since the incident at Wounded Knee in the late 70's have been ramped there even more so than ever before. Now there is a greater need for more security and funding to help Native Americans achieve self-determination on reservations.   In the third article "Justice Department focusing on Indian country crime" by Carries Johnson this article focuses primarily on the reservation itself. With a bill submitted for congress so more grant money for "Youth mentoring, victim assistance and crime prevention" can be allotted to reservations so "workers responsible for policing crime on the reservations".

The American Indian Movement (AIM) was formed "to oppose the intense poverty and racism Native Americans faced". In the fourth article by Robert Siegal "Peltier parole prospects spurs debate" as well during this period of time to control and police the reservations but more violence and deaths have occurred".   Two FBI agents were killed and several bystanders were also killed in the shot out on the Pine Ridge reservation which lead to arrest of Leonard Peltier who is incarcerated for those deaths. Pending a parole hearing he may see to live the rest of his life back on the reservation in which he was sworn to protect, because he knows who really killed those men and hopes that one day that person will confess so he can see some of his family who has been waiting patiently for his release.

Established in the 1789-1824's the bureau of Indian affairs first was in the war department and it was a separate bureau; 1849 it was changed to the U.S. Department of the Interior. They handled trade with Native American's; administration conflicts lead to The Dawes Act of 1887, The Burke Act of 1906, and the Wheeler-Howard Act of 1934 and now they just act as trustee over Native American lands and funds. AIM members drove a caravan to Washington DC in the early 70's and took control of the BIA offices they ransacked and destroyed ancient artifacts in protest of the bureau for that mishandling of their funds. Two million dollars' worth of artifacts that were taken from Native American was destroyed by them; office equipment was destroyed as well and was replaced.

With the establishment of laws that protect their rights as sovereignty nation so they can govern themselves are as follows:

> *The Dawes Act of 1887*-Provides land parcels to tribes and "Indian societies must and can be regenerated", another quote is "Status, responsibility and power", "Cultural and religious liberty" and that their lands must be "Used and cherished on the way the particular Indian groups desires"
>
> *The Burke Act of 1906*-Established citizenship

<u>*The Wheeler-Howard Act of 1934*</u>- Authorized tribes to draft
constitutions setting up the machinery of self-government
and of Incorporation to carry on tribal economic enterprises.

When a person is told over and over again that they will never be any good we tend to believe in just that.   But not for indigenous people their strength is in the massive that thrive and that have survived the ongoing racism that still exists today. In Dr. Becky Slaton's power point presentation on "The Psychology of Prejudice: How stereotypes affect our thinking, beliefs and behavior" she teaches us that if people of race are what they claim to be we as <u>Observers-expectancy</u> (Robert Rosenthal/Lenore Jacobson) should be able to spot the "Social Categorization" of certain groups. How social groups behave and act as part of the typical stereotype that we have been told throughout history.   Names such as "Lazy, Alcoholics and Gullible" are just a few that have been given to Native Americans throughout the centuries since Columbus landed.

A negative expectation of someone is what we want to think, forget the positives that this person has done. Once we have concluded from <u>Observers-expectancy </u>is confirmed in our own mind without even asking or finding out what exactly is the truth; we are satisfied with our own beliefs that this must be true. Of course individuals will however hide the truth from us because of the tendency to believe that some "whites" are there to steal their traditions and use them as if they were their own; and in many cases it is true.   The "Whites" who will do this are only out to make a profit off of the American Indian but by protecting the traditions that were handed down from generation to generation Native Americans can preserve their heritage and traditions.

Stereotyping has been done and still goes on every day, can individuals stop stereotyping altogether? The answer is yes.

This list of behaviors will cause an individual to become more self-identifying for their own life ways. #1 Do not jump to conclusions when seeing stereotype behavior from individuals #2 Don't behave the same way as the person who you are in the company of the person behaving stereotypical #3 Do question what is going on and why they are acting that way #4 Do respect the individual traditions and behaviors in which they are acting #5Do not try and repeat what the individual group is doing, that is their traditions not yours #6 Make sure that you ask permission to touch the scared object or participate in the event that is going on. This list is of my own doing and is only what I have learned from being around indigenous people for more than three years.

What are the services that are provided on the reservation by the government so Native American can help them better their own lives? On the reservations and in urban America the government provides health care for Native American, in fact educational programs and scholarships are available to everyone more so to minorities than any other group. According to the article "Indian health bill gain steam again" by Rob Capriccioso time is running out on new legislation to revitalize the Indian Health Care Improvement Act, which provides health care services to Native Americans and Alaska Natives "to help fulfill the U.S. government's treaty and trust responsibilities to Indian country" Which by my standards are long overdue.

This proposed bill will do the following: Authorize programs to increase the recruitment and retention of health care professionals, such as updates to the scholarship programs, demonstration programs which promote new, innovative of health care, to improve access to health care for Indians and Alaska Natives. Authorize long-term care, including home health care, assisted living and community based care. Current law provides for none of these forms of long-term care.   Establish mental and behavioral health programs beyond alcohol and substance abuse, such as fetal alcohol spectrum disorders, and child sexual abuse and domestic violence prevention programs. Establish demonstration projects that provide incentives to use innovative facility construction methods, such as modular component construction and mobile health stations, to save money and improve access to health care services. Require that the IHS budget account for medical inflation rates and population growth in order to combat the dramatic underfunding of the Indian health system.

With the establishment of the Native American Languages Act in 1990 and I quote "To preserve, protect and promote the rights and freedom of Native Americans to use, practice and develop Native American Languages" (Wikipedia).   Along with sacred feasts and ways of life the Mohawk are bringing not only their food but their language, knowledge and their love of community spirit (La Duke). The Indians of the northwest speak a great variety of languages, more than any other in its region at least forty-five different languages many like our own language of English take on a variety of different dialects, some even did not make very much sense. Also it gives Native Americans a sense of where they have come from, the land in which they were born on and a sense of who they are and what culture they were born into. It is the culture in which can be destroyed by not practicing the traditions that were handed down to a person and then passing it onto the next generation of children that come into this world.

But no longer, a movement is underway to bring back those sacred rights that have been taken away from them change was under way as early as the 1930's, bilingual programs were established, but it was the "Rough Rock School" (La Duke) in a remote Navajo-speaking district in 1966 that launch the indigenous nation to bring languages back into their world.   There are also "Super Families" (La Duke). of California which make up of over five to six families to which their dialects take upwards to 113 different meanings, which have both male and female combinations in them (La Duke).   Sign language was the beginning of the world for indigenous people they had to use different methods both with their hands and drawing pictures in the dirt as a form of communicating.

Since the new and more advanced technology the game called "Rez World" is billed as the first fully immersive 3-D interactive video game that can help young Indians learn to speak their own languages via a unique speech recognition component (Indian country article). This is going to be an awesome tool to get children and adults alike to learn their native language and to make it fun to do so children who are deep rooted into main stream society will catch themselves and realize they are learning something rather than playing a game and who knows they might want to learn more about their heritage and culture as well. Elders who do not know how to use the technology can be easily be taught by simply watching and interacting with the characters that fill the screen. Kind of like a wii game where a person is interacting with the golf lessons and bowling games that are on the screen.

Preservation means to keep something safe and to keep it alive for generations to come.   In today's indigenous language there are tribes who are beginning to bring back their own language on their reservations. Like the Sioux or the Lakota language which is a "Living language" that is practiced throughout North and South Dakota.   Radio stations broadcast entirely in their own language.   The Caddo are using song and dance to revive their own language.   Nations like the Mandan and the Lenni Lenpe are threatened with extinction (1).   Although three of the Lenni Lenape groups have crossed the border to Canada to preserve their dialects more than any of the other ones; some of the elders may remember part of their own language but Michael Black bull cannot be sure of that.

In the article *"Immersive video game aims to revitalize American Indian Languages"* by Indian Country today of the three groups that were established "A website of vocabulary" which the words were spelled out in roman script.   It also included elementary lesions in audio feature so children can hear the words being pronounced. In today's indigenous communities "Now in most tribes the pool of fluent speakers has been to a handful of elders" (1) it describes the tragic loss of something that was so powerful in the indigenous world that if it continues to be lost the language that was spoken so long ago will never come back to the native nations of our country. Loss of Languages is a serious thing and that the revival of it is growing rapidly but there has been a decline, most in part by indigenous people who now live in the cities and their children who know nothing of their heritage and background will lose out on precious traditions, such as their native language.

Revitalization of Native American Languages "To lose something is to gain it back" because what they have to offer is the spirit of their culture and the tradition's that were handed down to them as children and from one generation to the next that in itself is the richest and the most powerful thing on this earth and no one can take it away from them. When you are young you are taught by parents about the culture which your parents have grown up in and that they will continue to instill those values that make up the person who they gave life too.

It is called "Cultural genocide" of who their ancestors were and what they left behind for the next generation to learn the lessons of the past, so they won't be repeated. But how could their language disappear? With so many nations immersed in English as their first language often times their own is not being spoken that's why it is disappearing. The knowledge to keep their language alive is on the verge of expanding beyond boundaries that Native languages will continue to thrive. Many indigenous nations will never let them die out or even be extinct because language camps that the Yuchi elders hold every summer for children of the Kauk-speaking nation are another way of using their language again. All these are proposed so everyone will have a chance to thrive in their community.

The health of Children, Women and Men are essential for life on the reservation if they parish then the richness dies with them and future generations will never know how rich they really are.   Although growth and development already exists it is progress that we as a nationally diverse nation have to continue to make this country what it needs to be in the coming years. Without the foresight of men like Black Hawk and Gall two Native American warriors who saw battle between the United States to protect their nations from being wiped out. Black hawk was the war chief of Sauks who are people of the Midwestern plain and Gall being leader of the Lakota tribe both fought to save their people, in fact if it wasn't for these two men Native Americas "would not be alive today to pass on the traditions".

With the Civil rights movements in Alabama to the marches in Washington on the war in Vietnam to all races wanting an equal say in how we live as people of this country. New movements were under way in that same time period in the 1960's to bring light to the situation of the indigenous people who were beginning to feel forgotten and left behind. It continued throughout the early 1970's and still marches today on campuses and the formation of Native American clubs such as the NAISA here at Fresno City College in 1975. Stereotyping of Native Americans is changing, to such names as Activists, Educators, and Social Justice Advocates. Today even greater men and women are making their mark where ever they can by lecturing on issues that face Native American's who are still faced with the same stereotyping by everyone young and old because there is still more that the indigenous population has to accomplish.

The Pygmalion effect is clearly our own actions to what others believe, while others actions counter our beliefs leaving us to a self-fulfilling prophecy which can be blinding. We need to check ourselves in the mirror before we step into the shoes of another; here is how I live my life. When I want to get to know someone I just don't go up to them and say "hey what are you doing". I first step back and let them be who they are, I observe how they treat others and how they make friends. I may even ask if I can tag along with them while they discuss their lives; maybe eat with them and make friends with who they hang with.   Then when I have enough I will make sure that when I part company I make sure that it is on good terms, because one never knows when they might need a couch to sleep on.

Genocide and racial attacks on anyone is considered to be the worst possible thing to do to a person or to a group of people. My first impression of Columbus and the Spaniards when I first read about them was hey what a nice thing to do to help out indigenous people. Not so true, because of what I have read recently, they were a very bad bunch of tyrant's who only wanted gold and to strip this land of resources using indigenous people to extract it.   Also changing the image of a group of individuals is hard as well.   We as a nation tend to keep the stereotypes as a comfort so we can feel better about ourselves. If we could come out of the same thoughts of what we were to taught by our parents who were handed down the same thought pattern. Such in the case of abuse, when a father beats a child that child is likely to beat their child and the history of abuse is handed down from one generation to the other. We have the power to stop that vicious cycle just by not giving into the prophecy of seeing that it is something that is normal.

Getting help such as therapy and other counseling services are there to replace the cycle of abuse from happening in repeated circles. Much to do with women carrying on the abuse cycle of their fathers repeatedly raping them that too can be stopped; But I am talking about life on the reservation and the people who when they go to ask for help. There is no one to turn to because the so called "Professionals" take ever advantage of indigenous people because they think that their services deserve a little more compensation (canary effect).

It is only because "White" men are working there and by little choice that is the way it has been for centuries. Until Native Americans themselves have moved off of the reservations and into urban areas of the cities.

Forced off of the reservations and desperate to find a ways to support their families, Native Americans have been reaping the benefits of the educational system and health services that are provided off the reservation.   All of this information has come to me by the way of "The Canary Effect" a DVD that I watched on how the government is silently and sneakily dismantling Native American communities and pushing them off of the reservation to take the land that is beneath their feet. But with the education and training that Native Americans gain in urban America, they return to the reservation with the knowledge that they have gained to make it a better place.

The future outcome of Native education is alive and well in today's society, because many more Natives are getting an education and are graduating. With slight gains in education according to the National Center for Educational Stactics.edu web site "Minorities will represent 39 percent by the year 2020" this is taking into account African Americans, Latinos and Asian Americans. The demographics put African Americans at a 12 percent advantage and Native Americans at 1 percent of the total population. Raising awareness and teaching young children that it is possible to attain the "good life" is a possibility. Again going back to the positive role models that play such a vital role in our society, we need to teach the young that they two can get a higher education and to dream of the riches that are out there for them.

What about the past? It still needs to be dealt with, because there are still issues that face Native Americans that have to do with what happened in the past. Mostly the treaties that the government signed with Native Americans What went wrong? I would say trust issues between legit land owners and the government wanting to take what is not theirs. So the government makes up over 100 treaties to be signed and then they don't follow through with one ounce that they promised. That's government 101, But what can be done to make the government follow through with what they promised in the past, it seems to be a tough situation one would think.

When an individual thinks about protesters such as John Trudell at the occupancy of Alcatraz, they remember how a mass of people gathered to claim what was rightfully theirs. Today a grassroots movement is under way called "Idle no more" This is a group of Indigenous people who want the government of Canada to make good on their promises that they have made with indigenous people of Canada. What this movement will do is to call upon the government to adhere to the treaties that have been signed promising to protect land, education environment and water rights. Idle no more if they succeed will pose a precedent that may lead to our advocates and activists to consider joining forces to make the government here in the US to adhere to what it has promised to our indigenous people. Who knows what will happen in the coming future of our world.

Where the Buffalo go "how science ignores the living world"

This article is an overview of Vine Deloria Jr. this is just like reading

one of his works, in which I tried to be as eloquent as he was. He was a

man that was well spoken and very articulate enough to draw the reader

into his stories. In the first article we read for a class recently on *page 8*

he uses the term "By Golly" which through me through a loop. I did not

expect for a man to use that term, maybe if he was raised in the south I

would expect that but, for a educated man to use it, it just threw me off.

Let me explain, an educated man such as him who can articulate such

passion when talking about his people and of the connection Native

Americans have with everything, threw me. I mean I at time can be very

blunt about a lot of things but with my educational back ground

especially living in the south I don't even say that. This article was

actually fun to read, or even hear a well-educated person be completely

human at times and say things out of the ordinary once in a while is

good for the balance of human nature.

I can only wish that I spoke so eloquently, but I can't, when I write is the

only time words begin to form. I stumble so much when I talk it's not

even funny. I could practice but no one wants to listen to what I have to say, well sometimes when I have something to say which is rarely. Me and my sister talk a lot when it is just her and I, we can talk about anything, but outside my family there are very few people to talk about anything other than school or work.

I don't belong to any groups or even have any group of friends, look I try to open up to people but they shut me out so I in turn do the same. I should not but that is just what happens, and I give everyone a chance, more than one to change and let me in. I know that I stay open to them, and I give them time to deal with their personal life or whatever they may be going through at that time.

There is a difference between having friends and knowing a lot of people, and I know a lot of people, so when someone calls me their friend it is strange for me when they say it. Because they don't really know me, for example one of my co-workers does that and she really doesn't know me at all we don't meet for lunch or go shopping together or anything like that so it is only natural for me to be the way I am. I don't think anyone really does know me other than what I present myself to be. Only my family really knows me for who I truly am, and the people I do let in I keep them close to me, I would do anything to protect them within my powers, whatever I have I would give it all to them to make their life better and they would do the same I am sure of that. I know how to be spiritually connected to all living things; I know that you have to have the Ut most respect for everything. For example, it was probably when I was fourteen I found this bird's nest and the mother had abandon four of her babies, I tried my best to help them but they died anyway two days later. The moral of that lesion for me was I should have left them alone maybe their mother would have come back to take care of them and they would have lived. I know I can't go back and rewrite that time, but I have left living things alone in order for things to work out for themselves. I have always tried to be a better person to everyone, and sometimes that hasn't happened.

I have also had to find out who I really was and for that to happen I had to relearn everything that I was taught. I had to empty out the garbage that plagued me for years. I did so by letting myself see what I had become, and I needed to find out who I wanted to be, in order to become the person, I am today. Believe it or not I have this overwhelming need to help out where I can. All my life I have had that ability and I have had only a few chances to prove that to anyone. There is a saying you "can't care/love too much" and that's sums me up.

Appendix

American History timeline 900 before the common era and beyond

900-1000		500 nations inhabit the continent and develop civilizations
1100-1199		The decline of populations of indigenous people's nations /1090-1100
1200-1491		The restructure of nations on their land/rise and fall of civilizations
1492-1599		The genocide of Indigenous People /Columbus era/Coronado/De Soto
1600		***The beginning of Settlement of whites on Indian Land***
	1607	James Town was founded VA
	1620	Pilgrims landed at Plymouth Rock MA
	1630	Massachusetts Bay Colony
	1634	First settlers to Maryland
	1642	English Civil War
	1649	Charles, I Beheaded, Cromwell & Parliament Rule England
	1660	Restoration of Established 1660 Church & Monarchy Charles II Crowned
	1670	First English settlement in South Carolina
	1682	Pennsylvania Colony Begins
1700		
	1709-1710	First large German Immigration (Palatine)
	1712	North & South Carolina became separate provinces
	1717	Large Scotch Irish immigration begins, first wave
	1729	North & South Carolina are established as royal colonies
	1733	First settlers to Georgia
	1739	Morris NJ becomes a county
	1754-1763	French & Indian War
	1763	Treaty of Paris-British gets Canada &most of land east of Miss River
✓	1775-1783	**1776** US Constitution signed/Bounty land warrants 1775-1855
❖	1785	Spartanburg SC becomes a county
	1787	New Jersey becomes a state
	1788	US Constitution Adopted/Georgia & South Carolina become states

	1790	First US Federal Census/Indian wars
	1792	Kentucky becomes a state
	1796	Tennessee becomes a state
✓	1798	Fleming KY becomes a County/US constitution became official
1800		
	1803	Louisiana Purchase
	1805	Removal Act to force Native Americans off of their land
	1810	The great Cherokee Massacre at Yahoo Falls KY
	1812-1815	War of 1812/War with Britain
	12/09/1815	White IL becomes a county
*	12/10/1817	Mississippi becomes a state
	12/03/1818	Illinois became a state
*	12/14/1819	Alabama becomes a state
	1820	Sale of cash entries begin all over the united states*
*	05/15/1821	Monroe GA becomes a county
	1821	US acquires Florida/Missouri becomes a state 08/10/1821
*	01/21/1823	Yazoo MS becomes a county
	12/11/1826	Troup GA becomes a county
	1830	Treaty of Dancing Rabbit Creek
*	1832	Treaty of Pontotoc in Mississippi/ the treaty of the Chickasaw/Robert Gordon was a witness
	01/09/1836	Marshall AL becomes a county
	1836-1845	Republic of Texas/ Indiana becomes a state in 1836
	12/30/1838	Newton MO becomes a county
	02/15/1839	Menard IL becomes a county
	1846-1847	Mexican American War
	1848-1859	California gold rush/1858 Colorado gold rush starts and ends same time 59'
	12/20/1851	Polk GA becomes a county
	08/25/1855	Jefferson and Leavenworth KS become counties at the same time/ Final bounty act of 1855
	1860-1870	Molly Maguire coal miners
	1861	Kansas becomes a state 01/29/1861
	1863	Bear River Massacre in UT Jan 29th, 1863
	1864	Sand Creek Massacre
	1865	Civil war breaks out
	1869	Completion of the transcontinental Railroad
	1875-1888	Westward migration Urbanization Industrialization Immigration, especially from southern

			& eastern Europe
	1890		Wounded Knee Genocide of Native Americans on the Pine Ridge Reservation, South Dakota
	1898-1899		Spanish-American war
1900			**The start of the 20th Century**
	1914		Ludlow Massacre April 20th
	1917-1919		US involvement in WWI
	1918		Sarah Waters-Gordon dies in Selma AL
	1929		Great depression begins/Stock market crash of 1929
	1941-1945		US involvement in WWII
✓	1950-1955		Korean War
➤	1959-1975		Vietnam War
	1980-1998		Regan was president of California/Skirmishes in Afghan/Gulf War
	1999		End of the 20th Century
2000			***New era of battles at home and overseas***
	2001		Twin Towers are destroyed in New York/September 11th
	2001-2012		US sends troops overseas to combat Terrorism/ Come home latter part of 2012

Family	State	MDY	County month/day/Year that they were Established

JFG	AL	12/14/1819	Marshall-January 9th, 1836
JFG	GA	01/02/1788	Monroe-May 15th, 1821/Polk- Dec 20th, 1851/Troup-Dec 11th, 1826
FG	IL	12/03/1818	Menard-February 15th, 1839/White-December 9th, 1815
JB	IN	06/15/1836	
FG	KS	01/29/1861	Jefferson-August 25th, 1855/Leavenworth-Aug 25th, 1855
FG	KY	06/01/1792	Fleming-1798 no month and day associated with the date
Fr	MS	12/10/1817	Yazoo-Jan 21st, 1823
FG/JB	MO	08/10/1821	Newton-December 30th, 1838
FG	NJ	12/18/1787	MorrisCounty-1739 no month and day associated with the date
JFG	SC	1788	Spartanburg -1785 no month and day associated with the date

FG	TN	06/01/1796	

Legend

- ➢ FG-Floyd Gardner-dad
- ➢ JFG-Jimmie Francis Gordon-mom
- ➢ JB-Jerry Dale Breazeale
- ➢ **State Resource book for genealogist**

- ✓ Reference to Dad's family History
- ❖ Reference to Mom's family history
- ➢ Reference to Jerry's family history

<u>**Reference**</u>

1. *"Immersive video game aims to revitalize American Indian Languages"*. Indian Country Today, 2010 Web. 23 Feb. 2010.

2. *Buzzle.com*. Web. 7 May 2013. <http://www.buzzle.com/articles/famous/native americans.html>.

3. Capriccioso, Rob. *"Indian bill gain steam again"*. N.p.: n.p., n.d. *Fresno County Library*. Web. 4 May 2013. <www.fresnolibrary.org>.

4. Cuniff, Meghann M. *"Police seek help in solving racial attacks"*. N.p.: n.p., n.d. *Fresno County Library*. Web. 4 May 2013. <www.fresnolibrary.org>.

5. Dalby, Andrew. *"Language in danger"* The loss of linguistic diversity and the threat to our future* NY: Columbia University Press, 2003. 160-161. Print

6. Gardner, Linda L. *"Civilization"*. Fresno: Research Paper, 2009. Print.

   - *"Pacific North Coast Indians"*Fresno: Research paper, 2008 1 Print

7. Hansen, Liane. *"Your letters: Native languages/Liane tattoo"*. *Fresno County Library*. Web. 4 May 2013. <www.fresnolibrary.org>.

8. Johnson, Carrie. *"Justice Department Focusing on Indian country crime"*. *Fresno County Library*. Web. 4 May 2013. <www.fresnolibrary.org>.

9. La Duke, Winona. *"Recovering the sacred: the power of naming and claiming* Cambridge, 2005 pgs 68-162 Print

10. Rosenthal, Robert, and Lenore Jacobson. *"The Pygmailion Effect*. N.p.: Wikipedia, n.d. Web. 3 May 2013. <//http://en_wikipedia.org/wiki/pygmalion_effect>.

11. *Scribd.com*. Web. 2 May 2013. <//http:scribd.com/doc/6601563/Native-American-languages/info>.

12. Siegal, Robert. *"Peliter parole prospects spurs debate"*. N.p.: n.p., n.d. *Fresno County Library*. Web. 4 May 2013. <www.fresnolibrary.org>.

13. Slaton, Becky Dr. *"The Psychology of Prejudice"* How stereotypes affect our thinking, beliefs and behavior, PH.D Psychology N.p.: ppt slide. 2010. Print.

14. Smith, Andrea. *"Soul wound" the legacy of Native schools*. Article handed out in American Indian Studies, n.d. N. pag. Print.

15. --. *"Conquest: Sexual violence and American Indian genocide"*. MA: Cambridge, 2005. 160-61.

Print

16.

Additional sources: Interview's

   I.   *Michael Black Bull* from the Lenni Lenape Nation, additionally he is Ottawa, Caddo, Sioux, and Mandan-Hidatsa

  II.   *Michael Konkle* –Student advisor to the American Indian Studies Program and of the Maidu Nation

 III.   *Dr. Bernard Navarro*-Professor of American Indian Studies at Fresno City College and of the Ute Nation

<u>**References:**</u>*Civilization paper*

Fresno County Library site: www fresnolibrary org-Online database for the following articles:
Johnson, Carrie" Justice Department focusing on Indian county crime"
Siegal, Robert "Peliter parole prospects spurs debate"
Capriccioso, Rob "Indian bill gain steam again"
Hansen, Liane "Your letters: Native languages/ Liane tattoo"
Cuniff, Meghann M. "Police seek help in solving racial attacks"
Smith, Andrea "Soul Wound: The Legacy of Native American Schools"

Research articles from the Fresno county library site database:
Dawes Act of 1887
Burke Act 0f 1906
Wheeler-Howard Act of 1936
From Columbia University electronic encyclopedia 6th edition the following articles:
American Indian Movement (AIM) Reference Entry
Indian Affairs, Bureau also a Reference Entry
     ⬦ From the video "The Canary Effect" mostly from memory
     ⬦ From the Fresno Bee microfilm –"Protesting Indians Hold Onto US Building" dated 11-4-1972

Followed by the article "Indian Protest Damage--$2 Million"
dated 11-10-1972 from my own research collection